REPORTS COME IN

First published 2022 by The Hedgehog Poetry Press

Published in the UK by
The Hedgehog Poetry Press
5, Coppack House
Churchill Avenue
Clevedon
BS21 6QW

www.hedgehogpress.co.uk

ISBN: 978-1-913499-13-6

Cover image © Oz Hardwick

REPORTS COME IN

Oz Hardwick

Contents

The Fine Art of Recursion

We've been here before, a family glued to the screen, tired but afraid of sleep. There's four or five generations – very probably more, but I lose track beyond my grandparents – and I've never seen so many moustaches or lace-trimmed handkerchiefs. I've never heard so much tutting or sucking of boiled sweets. There's a knock at the door but no one answers. At a certain point the screen becomes nothing but an abstract composition of light and shade, a grisaille field with scarlet scars scraped into suggestive curves. There's a knock at the door but no one answers. Languages and their simultaneous translations explore antiphonal and harmonic possibilities that touch the gut more than heart or head, and we join the chorus with nodding and tears, nodding and tears, tutting and sucking at boiled sweets. Moustaches are stroked and eyes dabbed with lace-trimmed handkerchiefs. I answer the knock at the door and let the old world in. It tells me we've been here before as it lowers itself into the last empty chair. The screen is dazzling white but we can't turn away.

Border Control

Guards in soiled uniforms patrol today's arbitrary divisions, stamping papers, checking likenesses, and stamping out dissent before it can take a hold. We return to the place you grew up – redeveloped into luxury apartments and empty shops, though lampposts and graffitied benches remain – to find the street roped off and blue lights flashing. The guard tells us that there's nothing to see, that there's nothing to recall in tranquillity thirty or more years later, and that we should probably just find a pub or an art gallery, give up smoking, see a bit of the world while we still have time, and maybe even settle down on the south coast and raise a family, but that we should definitely leave before he's obliged to stamp our hands into useless stumps. The stains on his uniform concur. A little behind him, a clumsy lump of human brain lies awkward as a dropped ice cream, still trying to remember where it parked and whether it turned off all the lights. It's just one more question that it's better not to ask.

Mandate

After the storm, the swarm; after the countdown, the cooldown. After the votes are counted, the crying starts, the lying starts, and the statisticians state the obviously false. There's a bullet in the chamber, ready to rock, and chimes announce bulletins at the top of each hour. Ours is not to question why, not to weigh the what and where, not to wear our hearts on our sleeves. There's an art to dodging the issue, an art to dodging bullets, and an art to seeing through the artificial distinctions between the two when bullets are issued like prescription painkillers. After prescription, proscription. Where the script is missing, we must improvise, improving our chances of survival with a ready store of lies and crocodile tears. After the statistician, the statesman, charming in his chamber, ready to rock, tearing up uncounted votes, vetoing the bulletin at the top of the hour, lying about the bullet in his obviously false heart, lying about the storm.

Reasonable Expenses

It's the party of the year, with envoys and A-listers brushing elbows and delicate conversations. Everyone's words are dressed like butterflies and even the most casual glance is a blown glass bulb containing orchids and rare insects. The entomologist sent his apologies, but an orchid is definitely an orchid and the famous smell of rotting meat only enhances the sweetness of sticky petit fours that circulate on the backs of dickie-bowed turtles. The conversation skips from Strictly, to sport, to climate change denial, and someone drops a bon mot that rolls like a false eye beneath a straining table. Gossip column inches grow in direct proportion to the length of lizard tongues that lick behind celebrity ears. All suggestions are reasonable by candlelight and numbers are exchanged for notoriety. Repercussions will be felt in private rooms and public inquiries, but now the band is tuning up and it's time to loosen buttons and kick off our shoes.

Levelling Up

Above this enclave of polite conversation, ribs meet like lying fingers, gesturing care for all our sad but glowing mothers, dignity for the men and women who tirelessly dig to the centre of the Earth, soft beds and widescreen TVs for the animal companions who never let us down, and loaves and fishes – vegetarian/vegan/gluten free options available as a matter of course, of course – for all our Biblical children. Voices rise like prayers and prices towards a glass ceiling that's been papered over with last century's good news, while here in the hall of mirrors, mirages and minor indiscretions, no one gives a f— for facts which are nothing but acts of self-representation anyway. Above the level of police consideration, bribes are meat and drink to sticky fingers, riffling readies over desiccated bodies which reach hopelessly for ever more remote control. Vices grip like predators in the long grass, out where the still-breathing bodies are buried in the foundations of a new, imagined empire. With sincerity sourced from Ealing vicars and non-EU puppet shows, and blood-stained fingers wheedling in polite contempt, politic voices pledge to be level with us, to do their level best to level up, to keep a level head when the ribs crack and the ceiling comes tumbling down. A pause for applause but they're already gone. Charity begins and ends in a tax-deductible second home.

Extinction Catwalk

Today in Paris, lovers are spent by the government, their die-hard hearts rolling from the tops of decommissioned fire engines. News comes at second hand, but decisions made in Spring lay a feast for carbon intensive projects, subsidising funerals for the senses. We are in serious danger and embroidered opera coats, activists in sequinned caps, spattered with fake blood. Today in Paris, we are out of commission, out of money, out of brush strokes and real-life piercings, drenched in intricate plumes and beetroot from a military future, out of control. The meter is ticking. Today in Paris, backstage activists rethink children, frogmarched in remnants of fuchsia feathers, jumping off ladders with the tell-tale signatures of Blade Runner and Extinction Rebellion, shiny gold lips kissing fit models into devastating consequences. Even loss has its limits. Today in Paris, black high-octane boots twist remnants of campaigners into waiting vehicles, chopping them up and punking them out, as police prepare to bring their directional concepts to life.

Breaking News

Since we are effectively restricted to three minutes, we must keep things precise, restrict all travel to within a single room, and reduce our communications to nods and small gestures. Our emotions should be expressed – and preferably felt – with eyes only, or ideally not at all. It is advisable to avoid reading, or to restrict reading to haiku and unambiguous warning notices. It is human nature to ask questions, so it is better for all if we leave our humanity to one side until circumstances change: please leave it outside the main entrance to your property, but do not step across the threshold. Failure to comply will result in consequences you cannot imagine. Imagination may only be exercised while sleeping: this will be rigorously policed. Because of the nature of the emergency, the police will be granted extraordinary powers to search on suspicion, to find the fault in all of us, to lift small objects by thought alone, and to arrest time. Since we are effectively restricted to three minutes, the authorities will accept no responsibility, but will condone futile sacrifices to appease residual guilt or fear if restricted to domestic kitchens. We are all in this together. There are now ninety seconds remaining: please nod to confirm your understanding and compliance.

Epiphanies for All

In the absence of clear government guidelines, I've convinced myself that angels are everywhere, offering certainty, reliable advice and, when I need it, a firm hand on my shoulder that just says I'm doing ok. Usually they're invisible, so I need to close my eyes to see them, slim and magnificent as a Doré engraving; other times they'll take the earthly form of a traffic warden or a daytime game show host. I don't know what I'm doing with my life so, as MPs sweat and bluster, harrumphing in the blowback from a million avoidable tragedies, I seek the comfort of catchphrases and fixed penalty notices, parking my car on the double yellows outside the studio and hammering on their pearly gates. *No deal,* says a disembodied voice. *For you the chase is over.* It's what I need and, reassured, I return to the ecclesiastical gloom of my ticket-plastered car. There's a tap on the windscreen, another fixed fine, and an angel in the back seat reminds me that I'm the weakest link. On the radio, the Minister for Innovation and Obfuscation promises epiphanies for all, free school lunches, and wings by next Easter at the latest. I'd head for home, but even the road markings are too ambiguous to trust.

Cracked

It's the last gasp and we need new faces. We need new eyes and freshly sculpted eyebrows. We need shiny new lips and tidier teeth. We need to be able to trust their innocence and rely on their enthusiasm; to know that when we look they'll be making all the right gestures with their foreheads, and that even in the dark they'll be pressing close, like party balloons in the back of a police van. It's the last throw of the dice, though there are no dice and our hands are too weighed down with money to throw anything, so we need new faces to sell to the public and to our friends and colleagues around the world. We need new expressions, like fish discovering that – not in the immediate future, but way down the line after we've all gone – they'll grow their own legs and bicycles may at last become useful. We need new intricacies of non-verbal communication, like frontline responders gluing themselves to motorways, or tumbling restaurants wondering when they became aquaria. It's one hundred seconds to midnight and we need new faces for when the emergency services fail to arrive.

The Last Campaign

Expect the unelected, the Three Word Slogan stamped across lips sewn shut with piano wire, the narrowed eyes watching you as you undress. In the engine room, illegal labour feeds the furnace 24/7, shovelling accounts and counterarguments, adding their own names to the archive of ash. At the Captain's table, fat hands carve each other behind their backs and rumpled snouts blow snow. Expect the inconceivable: the stones and shit of the Ship of State snapping its moorings like the good old days, buying the world with beads and deeds, hammering its flags through the hearts of its new best friends. Big Brother's too busy trying on elaborate uniforms to watch anyone, raiding the dressing up box for plumes and more brocade, checking his reflection in the shine of his own esteem. Expect the unconscionable, the press of bodies in the steerage, the requisition notice stapled to bleeding skin, the rows of gleaming medals on the slaughterman's apron.

Test Drive

Pursuing fashion, I've bought myself a gun, which I keep in the glove box of my nondescript car. I don't need a gun, but then I don't need a car, though it's good to know they're waiting on the driveway in case circumstances shift. In the old days it was just fat cops, talking the talk as they waited outside downtown down-at-heel brownstones, but you can't even trust the weather these days, so you need to be prepared, and everyone on TV and online has a gun and a car. It's best to be unobtrusive and only go out in the twilight, when everyone has somewhere else to be, though they're only extras on an hourly rate that I'm sure I've seen before. Maybe they were in ads for guns or cars, and I'm almost sure I recognise those hands from close-ups of sexy stick shifts and triggers. I don't do faces, but I know satisfaction when I see it, and there's no hiding the softening of edges at the purr and click of guns and cars as their temperature eases implacably higher. Think kids at Christmas or families reunited after years apart. I follow fashion like a buzzard follows a wounded deer. Think gathering in silence round a tree or a bedside. Someone I half recognise stumbles and the weather changes before they hit the ground. Think petrol station flowers as a car pulls away, its glove box snapping shut.

Everything but the Dog

The city shrinks to models and decorations, the kinds of things you'd see on elaborate cakes or in a shop window. If you look close, you can see figures moving: two veiled women play tennis in a square where a fountain plays over stone angels; a masked and caped toddler tests his strength by lifting a school bus above his head, and a scrawny dog chews at – no, you don't want to look that close, so close your eyes and listen. An ice cream van chimes Bartók on a tired tape; a lamb-voiced child bleats for her lost mother; a sweating butcher sings the Bridal Chorus from *Lohengrin*, and a scrawny dog – no, it's that dog again, so close your eyes and lower your face to the tiny, tiny city. Feel the cold roofs and spires prickling your cheek. Feel the warmth of hopeful hands exploring your eyelids and the corners of your mouth. Feel that scrawny dog – because, whether you want to or not, you will always feel that scrawny dog scratching beneath your skin.

The Day After

It's always the day after something: anniversaries, elections, terrorist atrocities, or flash sales. There's a temporary screen in the town square that I think is for sport, but when I get closer it's showing the procedure for if a gunman opens fire. *If you are able to evacuate, get as far away from the danger area as possible* ... An ellipsis like a held breath, or the heartbeat you will to stop for fear it may be too loud. *The police may be unable to distinguish you from the attacker, they may treat you firmly* ... A new ellipsis the weight of panic, the weight of a small rucksack, the weight of off-the-record accounts the day after a failed bombing attempt. *Include anything else you think is important.* A full stop, uncompromising, a hollow point through presumed guilt. It's the day after escalated uncertainty, a distant relative's birthday, the unrecorded loss of a refugee boat, a charity dinner for old Etonians, a party in the park, a longer queue at the food bank. *Stop others from entering the area.*

The Pride of Liars

Where does pride go after the fall? Take, for example, a prince with a price on his head, with a monster under his bed, and with a sweat-stained shirt that he swears he's never seen before. Or a public schoolboy with a lopsided tie, a lopsided grin, wine-sour breath, and blood on his cynically clapping hands. What happens when the crown slips and the glass breaks, when the escort's fingers – can I say *escort*? can I say *fingers*? – when the escort's fingers are twitchy on their triggers, when the bigger picture intrudes with its skeletons in closets and cabinets, and its bone-dry contracts signed with false names in bodily fluids? Can I say *bodily fluids*? So, what happens when the rug's pulled, the sheets are tugged aside, and pride twists in the air like a handful of mirrors reflecting smug buggers' faces and the inevitable smash of a lifetime of bad luck for all concerned? Take, for example, the haunted eyes of the weakest of the pack, his back stabbed by those who once stroked or scratched. Then, take down these flags to burn through the long winter nights. All fall down. All fall down. Pride is thin, sick smoke at nightfall, long after mirrors have been swept away.

Souvenirs

We live in the snow globe with flimsy buildings, our eyes bright with glitter and our lungs slow with glycerine and antifreeze. We're a scene from a city that's been scrubbed from the map, its streets lined with bricks and boots, its bones stuck raw through scorch-black walls. It's a city fissuring beneath a tightening glass sky, a breathless bubble purposed for storms, a nexus of trembling hands that shake dead space into brief terrors. A woman in coat as red as a fairytale circles a scarred square, dragging a basket full of children who cry in the cold like a cracked carillon struck by sharp hammers. Mosques and museums, churches and chain stores, are little but stories on flimsy paper and frozen tongues. *Fi-fi-fo-fum:* glitter in the air and poison in our lungs. The city shakes like plaster roses.

Pictures at an Exhibition

Reports come in of a ripped city and a painted sigh, a pained sky, a tainted cup passed from lip to lip as ships pile up until they block out the sun. Reports come in of a running child trailing grey rags, stray flags, flayed skin streaming like a river, or a ribbon, or a roll of dirty bandage unwinding from a wound. Reports come in of trembling foundations, troubling privations, tumbling divides of dry skin and sinew slit from faces that look just like yours or mine but which could not be identified beneath ash and brick dust. We have learned not to trust the evidence of gouged eyes. We have learned to be sceptical of split tongues. We have learned to ignore the broken hand that tugs at our sleeve and gestures towards towns torn from picture books and erased by fire. It's time to leave but reports come in that we're trapped in a burning house, in a city we've never heard of, and in all this time we've learned nothing but smoke.

Versions of several of these poems first appeared in *International Times*.

For those ground down & those who will rise.

Oz Hardwick has published nine full poetry collections and chapbooks, most recently *Wolf Planet* (Hedgehog, 2020), as well as countless individual poems in international journals and anthologies. He has performed and held residencies in the UK, US, Europe and Australia. With Anne Caldwell, he has edited *The Valley Press Anthology of Prose Poetry* (Valley Press, 2019) and *Prose Poetry in Theory and Practice* (Routledge, 2022). Oz is Professor of Creative Writing at Leeds Trinity University and has also published widely on medieval art and literature, and on medievalism.

CPSIA information can be obtained
at www.ICGtesting.com
Printed in the USA
LVHW101942100622
720908LV00003B/146